Lay Down
&
Get Lost

Nikola Pepera

For Andrew & Lizzie
Young & Vulnerable Poets

ALSO OUT ON FAR WEST

farwestpress.com

+1 (541) FAR-WEST

Darkness Is A Rainbow

On Our Bad Days
We are all
Abalone Shells
Reflecting The Sunlight
Off Eachother
As Intolerable Rainbows

And On Our Good Days
We Blind Eachother
With Such Reflections
And
Revel In The Darkness

Psychedelic Prostitutes

Wear me Out to Marmalade Birdie's
No More Bad Juju for You
For You
No More Bad Juju for You

Wear me out to the Harem
I am your Drink Me
Wear me out to the Dance
Mulungu
Saffron
Lilac
When Fools Attack
One more chance
One Fingernail of Philosophy
And Bring to the River Seine
All of your Tears

Psychedelic Prostitutes like Us wear white Go Go
boots
Out to the Oyster Bars On The Beaches of Mars
A Love Story
His Venus is Conjunct Her Sun
Her Skirt is Mini
He Remembers their time in the Biba Shoppe
Getting toast in her Hair
Marmalade Birdie She makes his toast so Golden
One Psychedelic Prostitute
Has Now Loved Like Never Before
And Loved as wide as the distance
Between
The City & In Forests

We smile at the Distance and Die

My Main Man
My Main Man

Lettuce Leaf
Leather
And
Lace
Sorrow
Sorrow
Why Not Tomorrow?

Coughing into The River Seine
Rivera Rats Sleep Deeply
Knowing
Their Value

Love & Chains
Bruises at the Wrist
Goodbye
Goodbye
Goodbye, Says the Walrus

Psychedelic Prostitutes like me
Live best near the forest or the sea
But a river will do
For Bright Rain
Such As Us

Rambling
Miraculous
Enchanted
In
Zuma Beach Sequin

Fill Me & Remember Me In your turquoise lace diary
Psychedelic Prostitutes Like Us Cry
Fast and Nebulous
In a Trance
Sleeping on Our Crystal Beach

Rubies Topaz and Watermelon Tourmaline
Let's Gamble

We've got all Nite
And
We've got Yesterday's Caftan
To keep away
The Reaper

Psychedelic Prostitutes Together Lining Their Eyes
In the backstage Cabaret Mirror

Wishful
Lips
Lurex
Carnelian
Carnation
Fuschia
Tarnation

Psychedelic Prostitutes like Us
Who knows where
We've Been?
Psychedelic Prostitutes
Who Knows
Where
We have Been?

Come Dance With Us

OH! How do I Stay Alive
I dance like a
Strawberry
Off her
Sunshine Vine

And when I want to cry?
I dance with
The Little Moon
And
The Big Moon
Too

Come Dance With Us

OH! How do you stay alive?

You dance like a
Pomegranate
And His One Thousand Seeds

We must dance
Away the Day
Follow Me into the
Dancing Garden

It's So Easy

The way
Love
Ought to
Be

OH! Come dance with
Me

Hippie Hippie
Hourrah

I'll put it on
The Stereo

OH! Come Dance With Me
OH! Come Dance With Us
OH! Come Dance With Us

Come Dance With Us

The Red Unicorn

In Tranquility
I Beg of Thee
Let Me Do
My Alchemy

Blue Butterfly
Vanish Me
Without A Sound
I won't
Climb Down
Invisible Moon
You Are My
Doom
Invisible Scream
You Are My
Queen

I am Red
I have Eaten
All of your
Fire
I have Eaten
All of your
Rage
Thee Moon Is A Liar
Illusion Is My Cape
I wear out to Sea

I am Porcelain
Foolish and Funny

I am The Red Unicorn
I am Doing Alchemy
I am The Red Unicorn
I am Doing Alchemy

Run through the Meadows
Of the Seasons

Hold Down
Your head
In The Winter
Feel The Leaves
Sing Through Your Hair
Orange
Cerise
Maroon
Umber from Under
Neary Lagoon

Laugh through The Summer
Dazed in The Sun
Slumber in The Spring

Now I'm the
Only One

My Astral Dream

I am The Red Unicorn
I have Destroyed You

I will now leave
My Forest
For The Sea

I am The Red Unicorn
I am doing Alchemy
While the Silent Stars
Watch Over Me

Have you been down
The Way?
Down Fountain Avenue,
To Charlie Chaplin's Bedroom?

Music In Thee Air

I need Music in Thee Air
I need Music in Thee Air
I need Music
To Drown out
The voices Of Evil Men
I need Music
More than I need
Air

I need Music
I need Music
I don't care
I need Music
More than I need
Air

That's why
You Hum
And
That's why
I Hum

We Need Music In Thee Air
We Need Music In Thee Air

The Groovy Part of David Crosby

We have lost
My Felt Hat that Jerry Hall
Wore In 1974
Burnt Cerise
But You call it Orange

I'm so disappointed
On the flight
Back from Florida
After Christmas With Your Mom
That David Crosby is such a Prick in Your Eyes
After you watched
The inflight movie show
If I Could Only Remember My Name

I'm disappointed
For Common Men
To find out that
Phil Collins
Was involved with David Crosby's
Liver
Why couldn't
Phil Collins
Save
My Own
Dads Liver in 1996?

I laughed on our Divan
Eating Rapini
I laughed above your guitar
In your Dashiki
I laughed at Jennifer Robin
Who lets me know
David Crosby donated
His sperm to Melissa
Many Years ago

I never knew

David Crosby would not finish his
Asparagus
You said
It was Roman of Us
To share it with him

It is still the day that David Crosby Died
But Jennifer Robin wears a Harlequins Revenge Dress
You Don't Have To Cry
Is about All of Us
I decide In my smudged eyeliner

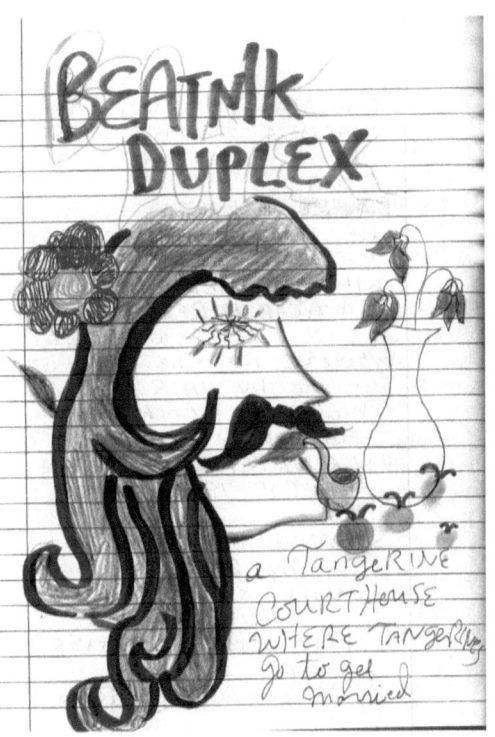

BEATNIK DUPLEX

a Tangerine
Courthouse
where tangerines
go to get
married

All My Husbands

On Tuberose Laundry Soap Wind
I am made wicked
Staring
&
Standing
In his magazine aisles
Of Romance

One husband for every
Two years of my adult existence
It's your math problem
&
My Philosophy

You live with the Men
You love
If you really Love Him
You Live With Him

Elizabeth Taylor has
Double Eyelashes
And less husbands
Than Me

And if you really love him
You'll still love him
When he is feral

All My Husbands
Day After Day
Nite After Nite

I'm out of his car and I'm up the street in
Patchwork Fur
Not looking back
My kiss I blow
She is imaginary

And
She never existed
because
He never blew it back

If you Love
A Man
You'll Live with him
And his
ShowBiz
You'll still be there
when he gets off the plane
From Daisy Detox
Or
Some other place
You never knew existed

Toxic Violets Scream
Gloomy Banshees
With Wigs of WinterViolet
I want to
Stop
Banging His Gongs of Romance

We could go swimming
And burn
A fire on the cliff
But only if I love
Him
More than
The rest of
All My Husbands

Gone Camping?
I won't go
Until we are
Truly Married
With Violet Ribbon
Given From
Thee Benevolent Gnome

Of Felton

On a Misty Mountain Top

You'll live with the men
You love

You'll Die For it

Scream Queen, San Pedro's Wife

San Pedro's Wife
Jangles In & Jangles Out
Of Your Boots

Scream Queen

Spider Trees
Horse Meadows
Gypsy Ivy Too
Pogonip Acid Trip

I'm All Alone with You

Moonlight is Your Only Lover
Tonite and Tomorrow
And without a doubt
Yesterday

In Godiva's Hair

All over Los Angeles
Bungalows Are Boarded Up
In Deep Green Plasticine
The 13 Floors
Are Coming For Us
&
Our Poetry

In A Dwarves Name
Jealous Roses
Pick Me
Their Thorns Smile
In The Snow
Melting

I Swim & I Flee
From
Sea to Sea
To A Castle
Above a Monastery
Where Monks spell out

A Rainbow

He Was A Dwarf
&
He Hated My Guitar
So He Painted Me Without It
He painted me
In his little
Dwarf Hand
In Onyx & Navy
So Tonite or Tomorrow
You'll Look At Me
Hanging from your Wall
Above your Bed
In Godiva's Hair
The Paint Dripping Down

In Dark Funny Red

He was A Dwarf

He was Smoking up
All of My Tree Moss
From a forgotten
Flower Vase
Him
&
Me
Slumming it
At Lucretia Place
He was a Dwarf
Stumbling & Strangling Me Until
He lost me
In A Labyrinth Of Emeralds So Green
While My Head Turns
In Exorcism

He was A Dwarf
    And now you know why
I Can't Repeat The Motion Of Violence My Sweet
Guitar So Often Requires

And Now You Know Why I need Them, Guitarists
Yet

    All of the Men That I Love
    Won't play their Guitars
    This Long Year
    Longer than Godiva's Hair

He Was A Dwarf

And He was After Me
First I am Yellow Dear
Then I am Orange Love
Then I am Red My Love
Then I am Hot Red

My Princess
And Before
I Died
He named Me
Queen of The Witches

   Nobody can decide
   About
   My Gravestone
   So now I am
   Shimmering & Shimmering
   Shivering In the Rain

Living With The Violets of
Death

11:22 Angelic Harmony

Let's climb
Thee Unclimbed Ivy
And
Braid It
Into our Ears

Datura is Hiccuping
You
Into My Bed

I cannot wake up

11:22
What does it mean?
Everybodies
Always asking
Me

Angelic Harmony

Flooded in on
Fountain Avenue
There lives a False Tangerine Tree
That my Eyes always
Walk into

Sign It
In Blood
In Desperation
With Sympathy
For All of Your
Unseeable Devils

See Me
And My
Playing Cards

You have left

All of your
Fools Turquoise
At the betting office
And all of
Your Money too
Your Turquoise
Falls Off of You

Energy Energy Energy
11:22 Angelic Harmony
What does it mean?
Everybodies always asking me

Young & Vulnerable Poets

You would have
Laughed
At the George Harrison
Memorial Tree
It's wood being eaten
By Beetles
In Griffith Park

I'm gathering
Mushrooms
&
Nine dollar Pianos
I'm gathering
Them

A Man from Movieland
Wants to crash his
Jaguar
Into Me
In broken English
Juanito comforts me
His security badge is
Rusting

More ugly hats in Pink
And
Muppet Fur Coats
Of
Glitter
Are
Glaring at me,
Glimmering

I'm tired of
Glaring
Back at them
I'm sleepy in
Paisley

Young and Vulnerable Poets
All Three of Us
Were
And are Still

My eyes are
Abyss
When I cross his path
His Parrot
Got Out
And he doesn't know
How
Or
When
It even happened

He's running down the sidewalk
So Manic
The same way that You did
After Me
The December
You
Shoplifted canvases
Just to impress me

We had plenty of
Money

Dropouts, not impressing
Anyone
Born To Lie

We were
Young and Vulnerable Poets
All Three of Us Were
And Are Still

All of The Poems
That We

Wrote
To One Another
For One Another
Because
Of
One Another

Somebody Ate them
And Never woke up

Degenerate Painter
In The Victorian Window
Degenerate Poet,
Victoria, Victoria
Victory
Swim with
Deep End Me
The Swimmer
Infinity, Algae

Young & Vulnerable Poets
All Three of Us
Were
And Are Still

Dracula Thee Frog

At Strangeways Prison
Christmas Trees
Are
Hooting
At Her
Owl Tattoos

A Kiss from Dracula The Frog
Makes no sense
Crack me Open
I Am your
Walnut Avenue Woman

At Strangeways Prison
The Owl Tattoo
Hoots back at You

Bars on my window
Birdseed or Roses
At My Boots
You have thrown them
A Sunflowers Apology
For growing too tall
To Kiss
Strangeways Prison, here we come
Locked up
Care of Cell 666
The Devils Last Trick

Kissing Dracula The Frog
Before
Your Wedding Day
Kissing Dracula The Frog
Before
He Hops Away

Lilypad Melodies
Acid Beret Runaway

Lost in Sparrow's Fog
You have got me by
My Hair
My Frog
We'll get locked up
Forever
For this laughter

For this Music

Strangeways Prison
My Boots
Will break on through
The Bars
For One Last Kiss
From
Dracula Thee Frog

Lovely Rita Hayworth Avenue

If we could just get you to
Rita Hayworth Avenue
And to Lee Strasberg
We could get him away from Tijuana
If we could just get you there
On Time

But He couldn't make it

Marilyn Monroe is laughing up a Zoo

Get into the back of the bus
With The Graduate
KooKooKachoo is more than a Walrus Song

How does it feel to be Loved?

Classic Men Of The 1970s, San Francisco

Most Men
Can't take care of
Sick Women

The way he did

Be Strong
Be Stronger
Than Her
She who has
Slept Under
A Stone
Nearly every year
Barely Dreaming

Dreaming In Those Valium Blues

Be Stronger
Be more alive too
Be one of the ones
Who got out of
The Zoo

He's been
A Man of The City

The way
Classic Men of the 1970s
Should be

He's been up to
His neck
In Machines
And Ammonia
Electricity
Glue
Oil

And
Screws
Windows
And
Plasticine
Rubber
Tar
Wrenching Me

He's been
A Man Of The City
The way Classic Men Of the 1970s Should Be

Del Shannon, On My Radio

The City is turning
Me
Into a Shadow
In Del Shannon's Poetry

The City is turning
Me
Into The Love-In

So why is the Rust
Of
The Golden Gate Bridge
Screaming At Me?

You lived in Painted Ladies
You lived in a torn up Dashiki

Drinking Tequila
In Golden Gate Park
With Them
Smoking Up that Moss
With Them
The City is turning
Me
Into Wizards Strawberries

He's come all the way out here
In Blue Paisley
He's come all the way out here

Just like Scott McKenzie

The City is turning
Me
Into Your Blue Eyed Fool

The City is Eating Me Alive
But doesn't even care

And can't get enough
Of Me
Of Me
Of Me

I'm almost at my limit
I'm backwards

My Hair is crying
On the floor
My Hair is in
Your Wig
My Hair is Vertical
And now
A Bowl of Ancient Cherries
Is finally
My Hair

You are getting
The Pits
Like Plath Did
Like Didion, too

Your Airplane Flies
A Sunrise
Choking on
Garbo's Smog

Carve Me Out
City
And Carve Me
In
Kiss Me Back
To Life
We Will Again
Begin

Del Shannon, On My Radio
Wondering
What Went Wrong

A Hare Krishna In Tangiers

Ivan of Wolf Totem
Had
Stolen
My white
1967
911 Porsche

He wasn't
Returning
My calls
Either

Everytime
I dialed
Him
Metallic nail polish
Would disappear
Off of
One of
My Fingernails

You drove me
Too Wild
Around
A Wine Country
Bend

You drove me
Too Fast
Through
Salem Wine Country

My Passenger Door
Flew open
I flew out
Into the Bends

White Lacy Lace

Your pale
Summer Face
Laced Marijuana
Cigarettes
Catch the Smoke
In my throat

I've been the
Wife
Of
The Green Goblin
And
The Faerie Prince
Too

In Violet Lips
They found me
In Horror so Innocent
In Two different
Flying Shoes

I am back!

Back from
The Palest Dimension
Screaming
Crying
Laughing
Screaming
For
Blueberry Donuts

People knew
You were flying
First Class
To Tangiers

People Knew
People knew
You shared

Saffron Rice
With Hare Krishnas
In Tangiers

People Knew

I found my own
Arms and Lips
Hugging and Sucking
A Stone
All alone with all of thee
Other Doe Eyed Fishes
Alive and Well
In Flower Villa Hotel
La Cienega Boulevard

OLIVES

Olives
Aren't
Tired
From having to explain
Who They Are
To all the new
Strangers
They are now meeting

Olives
Aren't
Afraid
Of Being A Dead Undiscovered Delicacy
Invented
And
Born
For Sensual Feedback
And
Pleasure

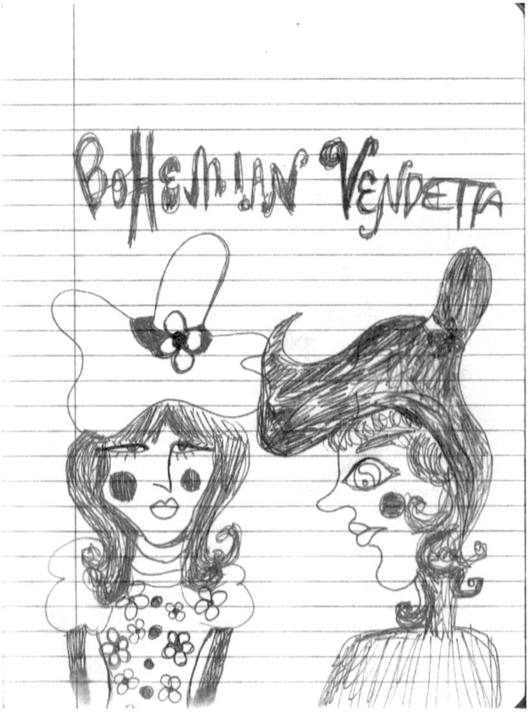
BOHEMIAN VENDETTA

Charlie Chaplin's Lemonade

Lay with Me
In the Red Mushrooms
On Charlie Chaplin's Lawn
At Patio Del Moro

Lemon Tree Truck Man
Has Wrecked His Truck
Before My Very Eyes
A Telephone Pole Fell
On Top Of His Lemon Tree

His Lemons roll on down Harper Across Fountain

Lemonheads Know a Place they can Go
They go Downhill

They take Lemon Tree Truck Man Away
Wrapped in a White Coat
Down to his Waist
His Eyes Laugh into Mine
He is A Tequila Worm Screaming into me
From The Stretcher
It could happen
To You Someday Too!
If you get Mad Enough
Mad Enough
About Lawns!
And
Mad Enough
About Lemons,

His Tongue Peels

If You Go Mad
On Fountain Avenue
Don't
Say Anything

Silence!

Don't Worry Charlie,
Here Comes Oona
Down the Way from
Chateau Marmont
A Bag of Lemons
In Her Arms
To make you Cool Again
To make you Sweet again

To make you Lemonade

Skyless Sky

Up and Down
The Horse Track
Racing Into Warlock Winter

Be My Racetrack Eraser
Erase Me

Men who want to be
Syd
But got wrong
The Orange
And
Blue Stripes

In your
Alternating Realities
He is a Witch
With a Wrench
Wrenching thee Abyss

Cannot you fix
The Stars?
So they hang aligned
Or
Hang Higher
In the Skyless Sky?

Men who want to be living
The Wicked Annabella Life
In Jennifer Gentle's Bathtub
Bathing In Violet Smoke Rings
Shoebox Dust
And
The Chrysanthemum Ashes
Of
Dead Mansions

You have not earned it

At your pretend concert
In mirrored shoes
She is watering
The Plants at Your Feet
With Grenadine

Troubadours
With that kind
Of Hair
Or
Stare
Are NOW Extinct
And Girls
Can't sell
Their suede scallop hem skirts
Fast Enough

Lolita, You Witch

She Sings
Midnight
In Mood Ring
Black

To Tell the Future
To Collide & Crash

In Surprise
She Sings Lullaby
To Black Afternoon
You Close Your Eyes
Under Her Palm Tree
His Secret Dakini

You are Elvira's Eyelashes
You Swim Backwards
Into the word
Wow
No matter what direction
You Swim
It's going to be
The Same

The Same

Lolita The Witch
Has come back
In the Nite
With One Eye Open
The Other Eye
Closed

Wink At Me
You know
How it will
End

Too Esoteric To Drive

White Smog and The Troggs
You with your 1968 Suitcase
Smiling in your Clowns Skin
Sobbing in The Rain

The Poppies are growing fat
In the Fields of Corralitos
From drinking all of your Tears

You wished that you still had
Guinevere's Corset
Or
An Orange Tree
Heavy with Peacocks Eggs

David Crosby has died today

Dearest Marc Bolan I am so very sorry
Your Pentagrams Vanish the Needle
For this Afternoon
We trade Your Unicorn for His Deja Vu

I am free and So is David Crosby
A Cat saw Me With You
You and Your
Mustache
Between his Teeth
Cats Teeth
If David Crosby were only a Cat
We wouldn't have
Guinevere

Tripping through my hallway
A Divorced Harlequin
I am Rageful
In My Peace

Nobody wants to drive us up into the Hills

So We Walk
I am too Esoteric to drive
And So are You

Marc Bolans
Walnut Tree
Is where I need you to
Bury Me
In the Springtime
When Harpies Howl

I am bored of your
Rose Scorched Castles
Trade my Disenchantment in
On Sunset & Fountain

His Peacocks Circle me
As I spill My Blood

I've told you
I am too Esoteric to Drive

And So Are You

Country Mouse, City Mouse

Country Mouse, City Mouse
Remember when
You lived on a beach

Gathering from your trees
Pomegranate Plum and Peach
Laughing In the Spider Trees
Where dandelions grew
Biting at your Knees

You are losing your mind
And you lose your keys
City Mouse, Country Mouse
Tear open my neck and drink
My Cactus Juice So Red
I cry Into The Mirror
&
The Mirror Cried back Into
Me

To keep away the Vagrants and the Beasts
Now, how much do we love
The Beach?

Country Mouse, City Mouse

Microdosing Vitex

Tho it is the second of
February
I do not wish to take down
My Christmas Tree
I'm Microdosing Vitex
On my balcony

I'm Microdosing Vitex
In a Taxi to the Beach
Remembering Your Hair
Full of Stars
And Tar
Your Hair
Where a Chameleon lives

Your Hair
Changing colours along with
Him

I'm Microdosing Vitex
I don't need any money
And I don't owe
You anything
Watch my fingernails
Scatter across and over
Your Keys
Violet Scream
Joker Green
Sea Lion Eyes
So Blue

I'm Microdosing Vitex
Without any care or caution
To History
Or what
You have Been
Died
And

Come back again as

Paint me as a Daisy
We are long eared Women
So don't ask me
I'm Microdosing Vitex
On the Patio of Stories
And
On Jim Morrison's Birthday too

I am microdosing Vitex
Don't ask me
I am unaskable
In Red Tights
Of a Pantomime
What can I do?
I've spent all of their money
On Stained Glass and Pianos
You aren't there yet
Where I am
You will be Someday
Microdosing Vitex on Your Balcony

Vincent's Blackberries

Buying Blackberries
You held out on me
In Hollywood Erewhon

Tonight is Friday
Christmas Lives
On and On

Vincent was out
In Aries Eyes
And feeling good
Wanting to meet people
Other people
Who buy Blackberries

I was by myself in mascara
And behind myself
In false eyelashes
At the Dry Cleaners
of Black Hearts

I will always
Hold it against you
That you, Camille Waldorf and
Vincent Gallo
Went to Cactus Bar Taqueria
On Vine, Not La Brea
Without Me

April Fools Day

The Kind of Woman I've become
Standing Next to You
Singing
Into your Abalone Bowls
Making Fried Oil Plantains for me

Saffron Musk
A Witch from Aptos makes in her kitchen
And A Black Leotard
I will wear both to meet you
At Seabright Beach
On April Fools Day
The Sun going down

The Moon in Cancer
Rising

The kind of Woman
I have become
With all of your Love
With all of your Lies
With all of your Laughter
The Kind of Fool I have become
Becoming The Woman Who Loves You

Mom, 1968

I was actually
There

Tonite She Lives
In Daffodils
In Sugar Water
Living Forever
Living Both

I actually touched
His Boots
In the Morning
And
In the Nite too

I was actually
There

Tonite She Lives
She's Living
In make believe
Mansions

I was actually there
His Guitar knew
My Name
And I knew
His Guitars Name too

Acid Beret

Street Names
Dance on By
Through My Eyes
And
Out through
My Sleeves

You are all Kaftan Casualties

Out from under
my purple fingernails
Debbie Doobie cannot
Suffer
Or
Swallow
The Wrath of her Mother
Every wine drinking rainbow I never wished on
Is Her Hair

To My Boyfriend
I Beg
Play Me
Once More
Your Daytime Lullaby
More of that Banana Album
Sunday Morning

Through A Hillside Village
Wearing a Crown of Poppies
And Daggers too
He has brought to me
My Head on a Plate

Is This Thee Mad Hatters Platter?

I will take a Tiger's Tail
And get burned again

I have come back
On Monday
My Door isn't the same
And nor is
My Paintbrush

Gypsy Girls like me
Go to the clouds off of one tea bag of Blackberry Sage

Paisley Haze Imagine Purple Haze
It's Christmas Everywhere in April
And
I've really lost it this time

Monterey Pop Mothers
Explain
Hand Me Down Seance Dresses
To Daughters

Light A White Rose On Fire
On Bloated Rose Paper
Blotter

!Oui! !Oui!
Mescaline Mavis
&
His French Sagittarius Lover

Living all alone
Off Oakwood Avenue
But Living Together
On Avocado Avenue
In Peace
In Tranquility

Him- thee Older Brother
By nine years
To Ecstasy Dave

Herbal Ecstasy
In a Pyramid shaped box

Have You Been Ever Dancing with The Flames of
Sagittarius?

Him-Very Cool
Through his Hair
His palm swam

Licorice Whips And Nag Champa
In Smoke In Sugar Coming off The Waves of My Radio

Dogs

Ever Since I went down to that Cactus Bar
In Hollywood off Selma
Dogs bark at Me
Like I'm their Living Devil

He Ain't Normally like this
Miss
I am so very sorry
Miss
And they Laugh too

At that Cactus Bar
A Vodka Vlad In Velvet
Cocks his Head At Me

If He could Bark
He would have

Venus and Dogwood
Drinking down his Vodka
He's a Liar in a Lake Sinking
Crushing Potatoes
Until they Bleed
How does a Leopard Burn?
Those Dogs Wonder
They watch from their staircases
Off Harper & De Longpre
Counting My Spots

I fly back to Egypt
In 1966
In My Leopard Skin Pillbox Hat
As Quiet as Leopards Purr
Sleeping through the Nite
High on Elderberry Sap

My Knock Me Down Man Is Here
A Crown of Candles

My Head going up in Flames
In My Fur, Cats follow me Home
Cats Soften to my Boots
Their Claws
Lover of Cats Claws down my back

Answer Me, Nite?

I wander that Cactus Bar
I stay in one corner to myself
Drawing Aphrodite Embracing Venus
In Green Diary Ink
Watching all of your heads thrown back
Taking your Shots

I drank some water from the Desert

Black and Whites strangled by vines
Of Raspberries

Red Wine Glasses
Break At The Stem Under Your Hand
And Dominoes Cascade
One After Another

My knock Me down Man is Here

I am not bleeding
Until tomorrow
And still these Dogs of Hollywood
Howl Into My Hair

San Francisco & Bolinas

Maybe we can get to the Reservoir On Time
Before the Sunsets
To Swim It
Swimming and Driving
As Long as the Porsche doesn't breakdown

He's talking me into
One Last Trip
With Him
Up through
Bolinas
Because He finally noticed
I'm 14 going on 27
And
I'm in Love with Brautigan

We all know how that went for Richard in Bolinas

Taking my photo
On the Lawn of the Palace of Fine Arts

You'll count the Clovers
And get A Lucky One

Thee Famous Court Jesters
of Felipe's Black Cat Castle

Stoned Immaculate
On the Grass Of Zenarruza Monastery
Faded On Basque Bill Murray's Hashish
You asked me
Do we sleep
At The Monastery?
Or
Do we sleep
At Basque Bill Murray's Castle?

I had us down that Mountain & off that Monks Lawn
I had us Back at his Castle in no time at all

Hash Wine Sin

Ten Days
Before that Nite
When we were lost
In The Mountains Of Orio
We shared our last Piel De Sapo Melon
The way Decent Muskrats should

And Two Nites Before that Nite

I hit my head
Laughing at you
On the pole of the train from Madrid to Saint Sebastian
With vending machine potato chips in my hair
I wish I could remember
What You said
To make me
Laugh So Desperately

You gave me the right kind of Dementia

Regret?

I will never regret
Using half of your entire Artistic Careers worth
Of White Out
On the sink of
Madrid Star Hotel
To Cover Up my hair dye stains
Or
Better More
To Erase all of Our
Mistakes

THE DEVILS UNICORNS

PHOENIX
BURN
BURN BURN

Hemlock Champagne

It's So Easy
To Talk
In Loud Circus Bars
When you're a Trapeze Artist
Flying through the Clouds in your Hair
And You can't come Up or Down
For Air

It's So Hard
To Talk
In Loud Circus Bars
When you're a Mentalist
Doing Cursive
In Frog's Roses and Butterfly's Ink
And all you can do is
Drink Drink Drink
Up that Hemlock Champagne

The Air That We Breathe
Played on the stereo

They photographed us
In Clown Bar Mirrors
Looking over our shoulder
And
Laughing
At how long it took us
To get back here
Back in Hollywood

Walk me blindly through
Canters
To her Cafeteria Sky
Grinning down on us
In Her Infinite Multiplication

Our Time Together In The Circus

Paradise Is A Place
Drawn on Your Neck
A Place For A Faerie Who Braids her Hair Down Her
Back
A Place For A Faerie
Sleeping On a Cliff
Your Faerie
She must Be
So Sleepy
Nitemares In Bellflowers
Pomegranates And Cream
Making her Dinner
Out of a Sunflower Seed

That's all that she could ever really Ever Need
Paradise Is A Place
For you to
Lay Down & Get Lost
In

Paradise Is A Place
The same place
I've bit into
During our time
Together In The Circus

Lonesome Hobo & Sentimental Hippy

Love Beads & Poetry
Doesn't mean that much
To me

I'm a sentimental hippy
A sentimental hippy

You had driven
All the Way
Up & Down
Pacific Coast Highway
Through the Storm of
A century
Just for a lock of my hair
To love you

Love Beads & Poetry
Doesn't mean that much
To me

I'm a sentimental hippy
A sentimental hippy

Hollywood Bungalows
Are full of
Funny lies
And
Pancakes in John Belushi's
Room
Are drowning
In Blue Sap

Don't let me catch you
Watching me cry
To myself
While the moon is
Broken in half

Don't let me catch you
Doused in Sap
On Fire
Your cap
Smoking all of
Victoria's Regrets
Like they were your
Very own

You'll find me anyway
No matter how I hide

Love Beads & Poetry
Doesn't mean that much
To me

I'm a sentimental hippy
A sentimental hippy
And
You Are My Lonesome Hobo

Love Beads & Poetry
Doesn't mean that much
To me

Wish Addict

After you love me
You are Splendide
Laying Down In Laburnum
And
Biting into
My Green Apple

After I Love you
I am Splendide
So You call me
She Devil

Parrots Surround You
Parrots Surround Me
Parrots all around You
Parrots Green Feathers
Parrots all around Me

We could take a Gold Line train
Back to Rivendell
I've heard the Green Apples there are full of
Moonlight
And
If you bite into one
Hard enough
You'll get a
Wish

Wish Addict
Wish Addict
Wish Addict

Is it really True?

What the Parrots are telling everybody all about you?
Or all About me too?
Have you ever met a parrot
Who is Blue?

He will tell everyone
All of Our Secrets

Let's Stay Together
Up high in the Green Apple Trees
Of Galadriel's
Singing Mirror
Where one
Bite of Moonlight
Will Fill Us
Now,
Wish

Burning Oregano At Steve Labates

Dolly Parton
Never Burned Nag Champa
In Her Powder Room

At Steve Labates Apartment
I sleep
On his leather couch
While I wait for
My Boyfriend
To Wake Up on Fountain Avenue

Dolly Parton would call me
A Stalker
And I agree with Her

Do you have any Nag Champa?
I ask Steve Labate
His Reply
You Hippy Fuck
Instead he offers Oregano

I wait and I wait
Waiting Waiting
For the Sun to come up
Waiting for my boyfriend
To Wake Up
On Fountain Avenue

I sleep in Dracula's Jacket
The one his
Witches
Stitched For Him
Down the Way
From Christie's Castle

But This Isn't
Transylvania
This is not

Musatesti

This Is Hollywood

I will wake up today
In Clouds of Oregano Smoke
Burning Away The Evil Spirits
Of
Monstrous Starlets who
Possess Me

I Will Burn Away The Evil Spirits
Pretending Steve Labate's
Oregano
Is
Dolly Parton's
Forbidden Nag Champa

Some Say It's Easy
To Be
A Hippy Fuck?

I can prove you,
It's Rough
In The Powder Rooms Of Babylon

Waiting Waiting Waiting
Oh What A Heartache

Yet Hippy Fucks
Like Us
Make Love Easy
Even
When It's Rough
In The Powder Rooms of Babylon

Oh What A Heartache
Oh What A Heartache
Yet
Hippy Fucks

Like Me or You
Make Love Easy
Even
When It's Rough

Waiting Waiting Waiting
In The Powder Rooms
Of
Babylon

The Black Butterflies

Arrange Us
In Our Crystalline Vase
And
In Hungry Leather
An Envelope
Dyed
In Lions Ash
Black

And when You come
Back?

Reach for my Wrist
And
Give it a Belated
Twist

The Black Butterflies
Are Back
In Season
With Teeth
Sinking
Waiting to Bite Us

Living Without You
Off Electric Avenue
With a Mask Of
Your Face
I paid a Sculptor
So Much Money to make

We can live off Lettuce
Just like
The Black Butterflies Do

Embers from Espers
I Dare You
We'll Fly Far

Ever So Far
And Fly Far, Far Against Time
Never to let it
Trap Us

The Black Butterflies
The Black Butterflies
The Black Butterflies